NATIONAL GEOGRAPHIC
KiDS

W9-BZU-154

# ON THE FARM
## STICKER ACTIVITY
## BOOK

Pull out the sticker sheets and keep
them by you as you complete each page.
There are also lots of extra stickers to
use in this book or anywhere you want!
Have fun!

**NATIONAL GEOGRAPHIC**
Washington, D.C.

Consultant: David Alderton
Editorial, Design, and Production by
make believe ideas

# Farmyard fun!

The farmyard is filled with many animals, from the cute and fluffy to the big and noisy!

Find the missing stickers and then draw lines to match the animals to their noises!

Baa!

cow

pig

Moo!

Oink!

sheep

Cock-a-doodle-doo!

2

rooster

Goats are good climbers. Some goats can also crawl under fences or jump over them!

goats

Help the ducklings find their mom!

Color the cute goat.

3

# Working hard!

**Find the missing vehicles!**

Farmers use different vehicles to help them with jobs around the farm.

tractor

baler

tractor and plow

combine harvester

Big, chunky tires help the tractor move over rough, muddy ground.

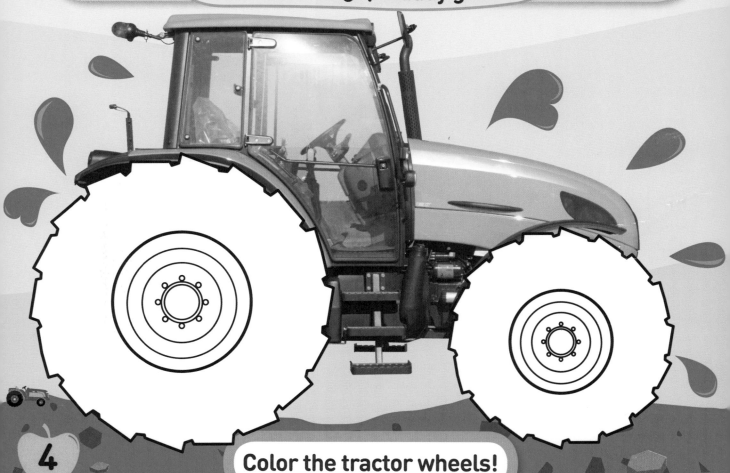

4

Color the tractor wheels!

Find the missing stickers to finish the patterns.

The combine harvester cuts and collects food, such as wheat and corn.

............. How many blue tractors can you find?

5

# Farmers grow many things!

Crops are foods that farmers grow for us to eat.

**Use stickers to sort the crops.**

apples    corn    oranges

**Start**

**Finish**

**Find your way through the corn maze!**

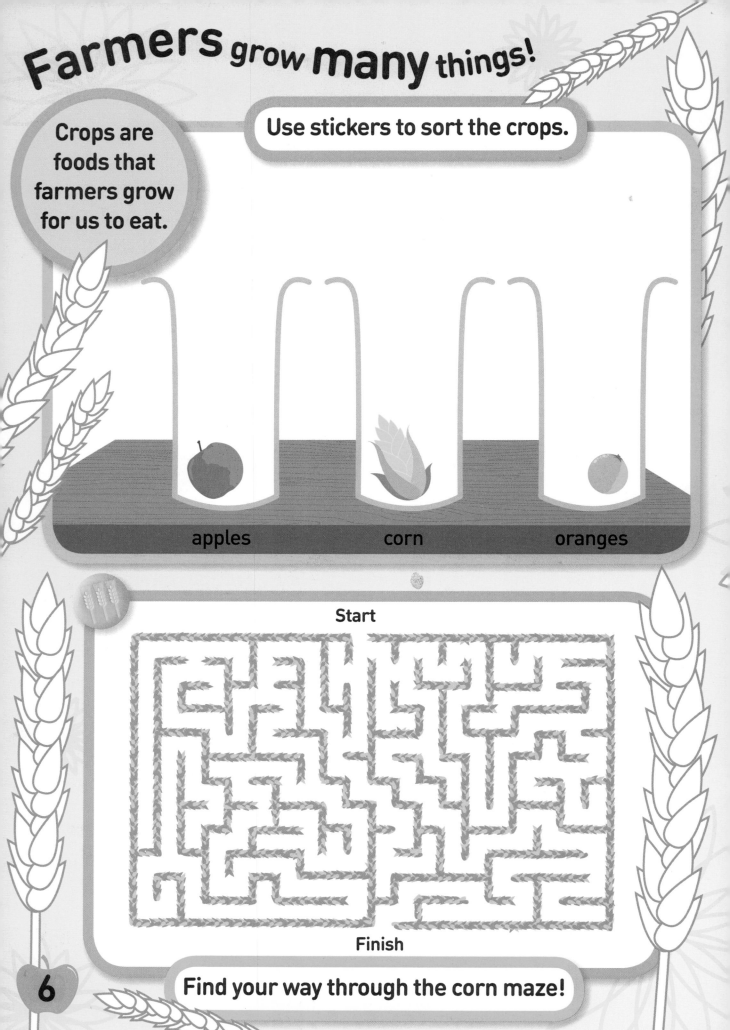

Some farmers grow flowers for our homes and backyards.

Color the sunflowers!

2 + 5 =

Add it up! Sticker the answer.

# Fabulous **food** and wonderful **wool!**

cheese

butter

yogurt

milk

Cows, sheep, and goats all give us milk. We use milk to make foods like cheese, yogurt, butter, and ice cream!

In one day, a dairy cow can produce around 128 glasses of milk!

Sticker the missing food and then draw lines to match the pictures to the words.

dairy cow

Color and sticker to make an ice-cream sundae!

We can use the wool from sheep and alpacas to make clothes.

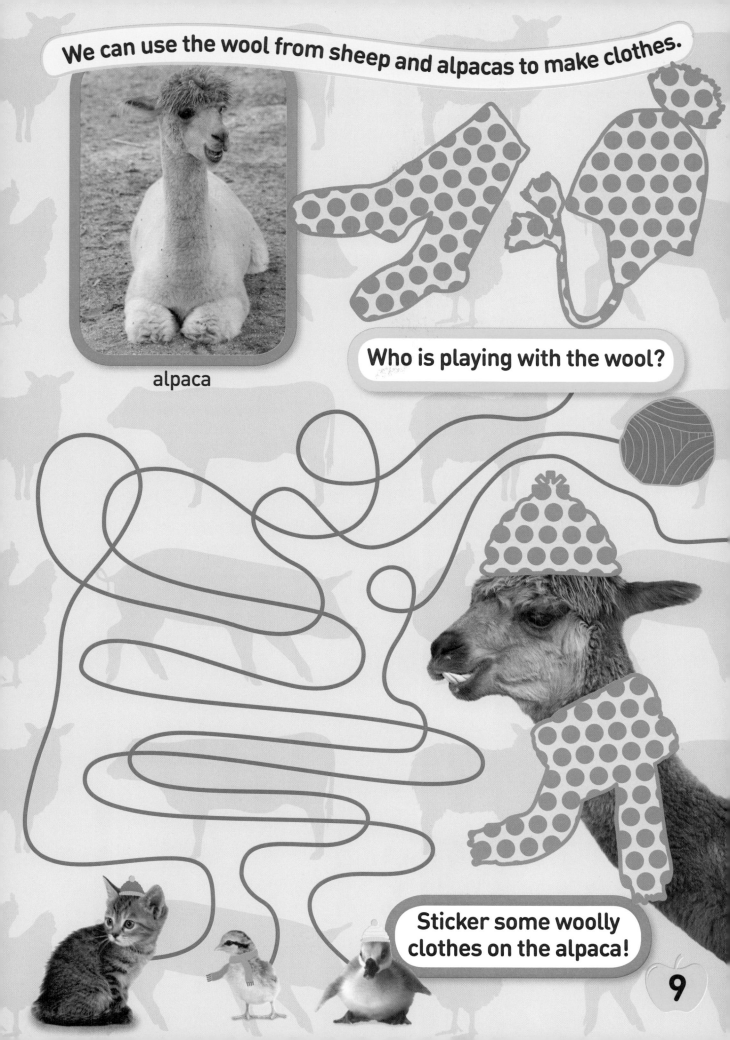

alpaca

Who is playing with the wool?

Sticker some woolly clothes on the alpaca!

9

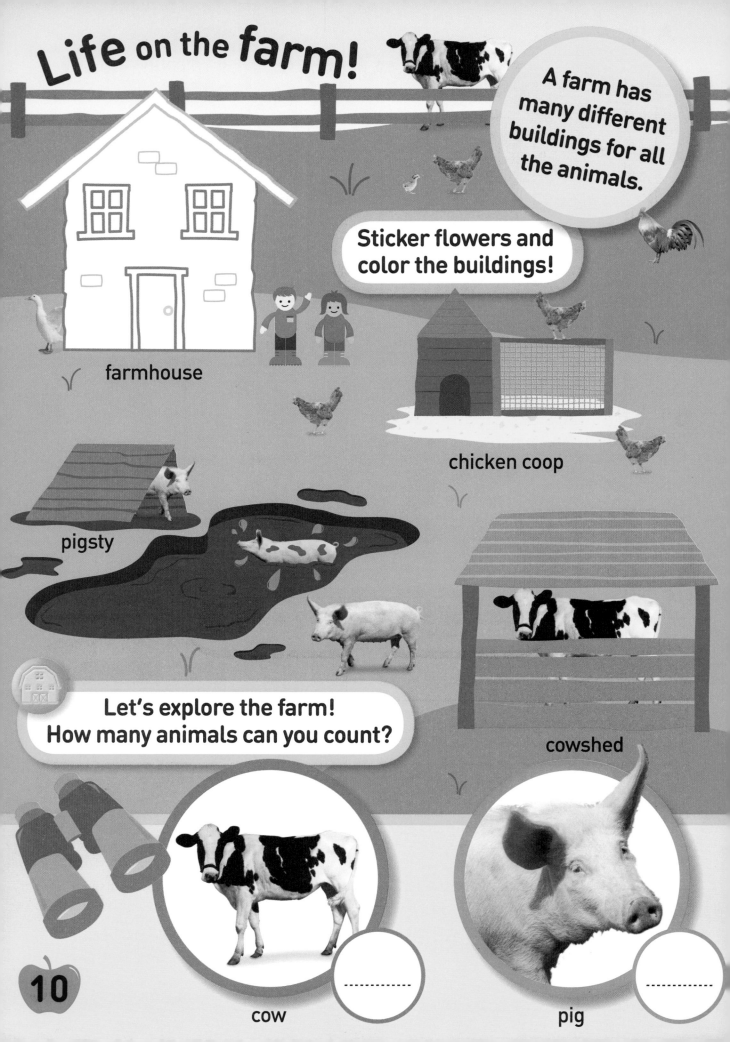

# Life on the farm!

A farm has many different buildings for all the animals.

Sticker flowers and color the buildings!

farmhouse

chicken coop

pigsty

cowshed

Let's explore the farm!
How many animals can you count?

10

cow

pig

duck house

stable

doghouse

barn

duck

chicken

11

# Meet the cows.

Farmers keep cows for their milk and meat. Baby cows are called calves.

Find the missing stickers and circle the one that doesn't belong.

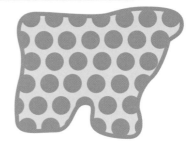

A highland cow's long hair protects it in the winter.

Draw the other half of the highland cow.

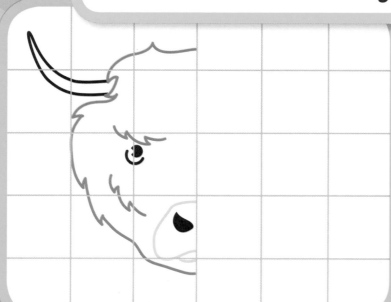

**Color and sticker the cows in the pasture.**

Texas longhorns have horns that can grow to 7 ft (2.1 m)!

**Sticker the missing horn!**

13

# Sheep graze in the field.

sheepshearing

Sheep spend most of their time eating grass. In the summer, their fleeces are cut off to make wool.

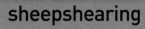
Help the sheep reach its friends. Watch out for the closed gates!

Start

Finish

Sheep like to stick close to each other. A group of sheep is called a flock.

Adult males are called rams and females are called ewes.

Find the missing stickers and circle the sheep that's different!

15

# Baby sheep are called lambs.

Lambs are born in the springtime. Farmers keep a close eye on them to make sure they are healthy.

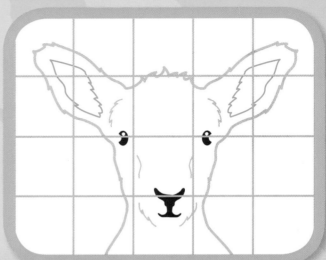

**Use the grid to draw a lamb!**

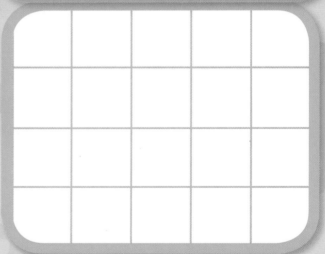

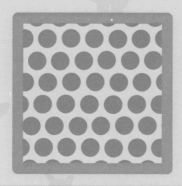

**Find the missing stickers!**

**Can you find five butterflies?**

Mother sheep feed their lambs with milk.

Help the lamb find its mom.

Sticker more flowers.

17

# Herding dogs round up sheep!

Herding dogs move and guide farm animals from place to place.

These dog breeds make good herding dogs.

border collie

kelpie

bearded collie

huntaway

Find the missing stickers.
Hint: The shapes will help!

People use calls, movements, and whistles to direct their dogs.

How many chickens can you count?

..............

Add stickers to help the dog herd the sheep!

Draw yourself as a herding-dog owner!

Color the trophy and sticker the winning dog!

19

# Pigs play in the mud!

 Draw lines to pair up the matching pigs.

Pigs are very intelligent. They grunt and squeal to talk to each other!

landrace pig

Oxford sandy and black pig

Vietnamese potbellied pig

Baby pigs are called piglets. Mother pigs usually give birth to about ten piglets!

Color the cute piglet. Can you give him a curly tail?

20

Pigs roll in the mud to protect their skin from sunburn!

Tamworth pig

Sticker pigs in the mud!

Sticker more mud splats!

# Chickens give us eggs.

## Meet the chicken family...

A male chicken is a rooster, a female is a hen, and a baby chicken is a chick.

hen

rooster

chick

comb

beak

tail

toe

| b | d | h | i | t |
|---|---|---|---|---|
| e | y | t | n | a |
| a | s | o | x | i |
| k | q | e | c | l |
| c | o | m | b | z |

**Find the words to finish the word search.**

beak • comb • tail • toe

22

Hens' eggs can be white, brown, pink, blue, and even green!

**2 + 3 =**

**2 + 4 =**

Add it up! Sticker the answers.

There are more chickens in the world than any other bird!

Finish the patterns.

# Ducks and geese splash in the water!

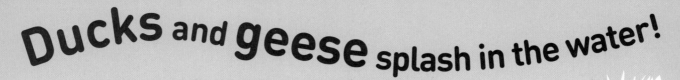

Ducks and geese are kept for their eggs, meat, and soft feathers.

domestic geese

white duck

With their loud honks, geese make excellent "guard dogs."

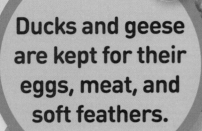

HONK!

HONK!

HONK!

Sticker a honking goose!

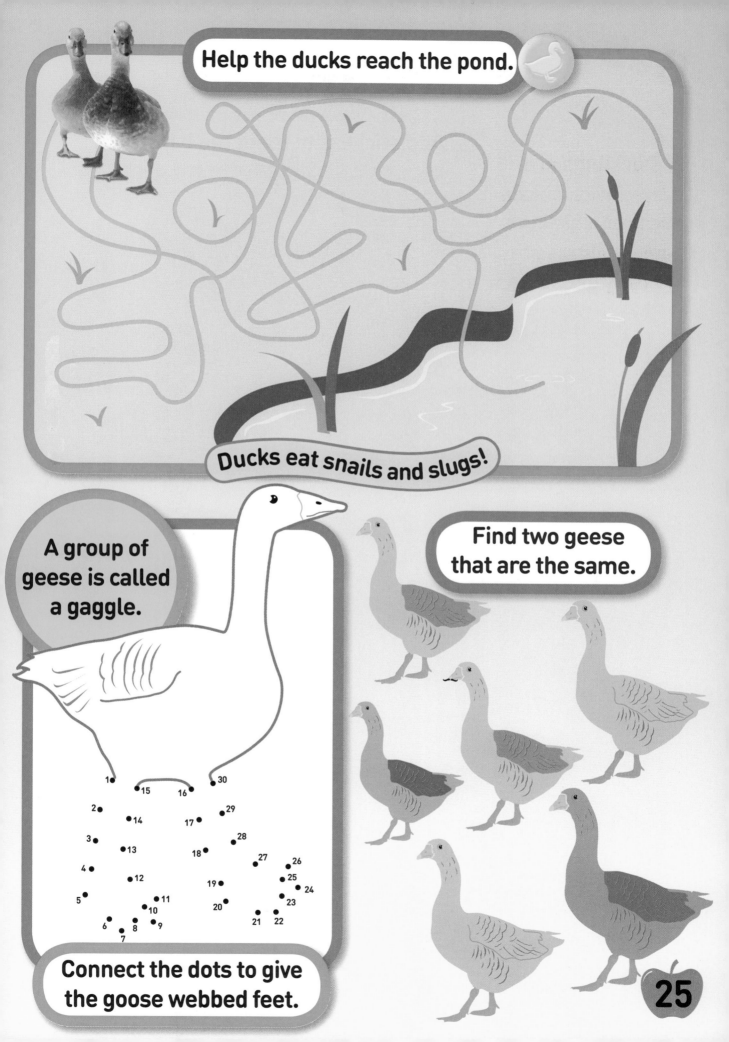

Help the ducks reach the pond.

Ducks eat snails and slugs!

A group of geese is called a gaggle.

Find two geese that are the same.

Connect the dots to give the goose webbed feet.

25

# Baby birds love to play!

Ducklings are baby ducks, chicks are baby chickens, and goslings are baby geese.

## Add stickers to meet the babies!

chick

gosling

duckling

## Find the missing stickers.

chick

## Draw your own cheeping chick!

Look for four differences between the scenes.

duckling

chick

ducklings

Find the five hidden chicks.

27

# Turkeys have fabulous feathers!

Turkeys are large farm birds. One turkey can have more than 5,000 feathers!

Give the turkeys more feathers.

Finish the patterns.

**Make the turkey colorful.**

A male turkey spreads out his feathers to attract a mate.

Finish

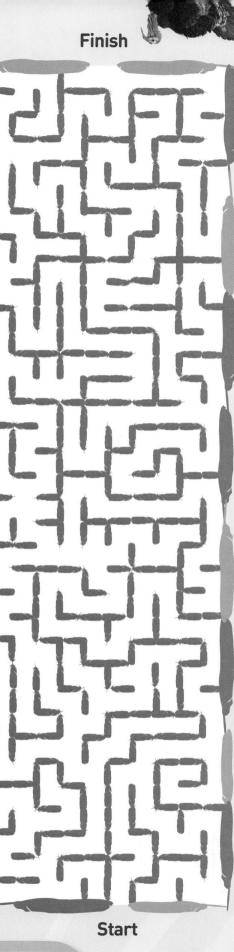

Start

**Help the turkey find its friend!**

29

# Gorgeous goats.

Farmers keep goats for their milk, wool, and meat.

domestic goat

Baby goats are called kids.

kids

Find two kids that are the same.

Add stickers to finish the goat family.

Both male and female goats can have beards.

Sticker beards on the goats!

31

# Horses are helpful!

Horses help pull plows, carts, and other heavy loads around the farm.

Belgian draft horses

Color the cute foal.

Clydesdales

Sticker the helpful horses.

Baby horses are called foals.

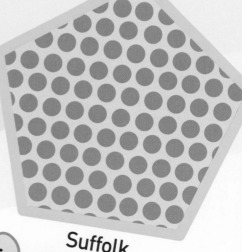

Suffolk punch horse

Help the horse find its friends!

Start

Finish

33

# Donkeys can protect.

Donkeys often live with sheep, cows, and goats to protect them from dogs and foxes.

What noise does a donkey make?

Use the grid to draw a donkey.

# Donkeys often groom each other!

## Color and sticker to decorate the donkey's home.

# Woolly llamas and alpacas!

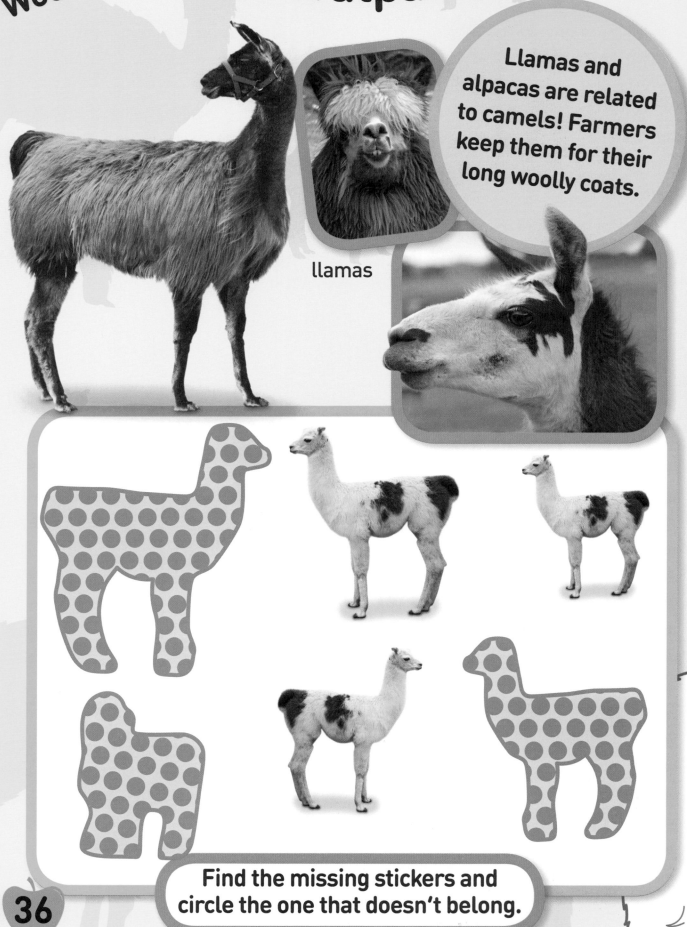

llamas

Llamas and alpacas are related to camels! Farmers keep them for their long woolly coats.

Find the missing stickers and circle the one that doesn't belong.

Some alpacas have such thick and fluffy wool that they look like teddy bears!

huacaya alpaca

Alpacas and llamas have two toes on each foot.

Sticker colorful footprints.

Color the alpaca.

# More farm birds, **big** and small!

Some farmers keep birds such as ostriches, guinea fowl, and quails.

ostrich

quail

Guinea fowl explore the farm for bugs to eat.

Which guinea fowl finds the bug?

Decorate the egg with stickers!

These eggs show you the actual size of an ostrich egg and a quail egg!

ostrich egg

quail egg

Find two feathers that are the same.

# My favorite farm animals!

**Find the missing stickers.**

**Draw your favorite farm animal.**

**Llamas and alpacas talk to each other by humming!**

Hmmmmmmmmmmmm